PRINCEWILL LAGANG

Navigating Singleness: Christian Dating for the Modern Age

First published by PRINCEWILL LAGANG 2023

Copyright © 2023 by Princewill Lagang

All rights reserved. No part of this publication may be reproduced, stored or transmitted in any form or by any means, electronic, mechanical, photocopying, recording, scanning, or otherwise without written permission from the publisher. It is illegal to copy this book, post it to a website, or distribute it by any other means without permission.

Princewill Lagang asserts the moral right to be identified as the author of this work.

First edition

This book was professionally typeset on Reedsy.
Find out more at reedsy.com

Contents

1	The Modern Landscape of Singleness	1
2	Navigating Singleness: A Season of Growth	4
3	Faith-Driven Dating Principles	7
4	Communication and Connection	10
5	Navigating the Digital World of Dating	13
6	Preparing for a Christ-Centered Relationship	16
7	Embracing Love: Entering a Christ-Centered Relationship	19
8	A Future Together: Preparing for Commitment	22
9	A Christ-Centered Marriage	25
10	Building a Christ-Centered Family	28
11	The Legacy of Faith	31
12	An Ever-Evolving Journey	34

1

The Modern Landscape of Singleness

In a world where fast-paced technology, evolving social norms, and an abundance of dating apps compete for our attention, the journey of navigating singleness within the Christian faith takes on a fresh and unique perspective. This chapter sets the stage for our exploration of "Navigating Singleness: Christian Dating for the Modern Age."

Section 1: The Quest for Connection

The chapter opens with an image of the modern Christian single, caught in the midst of the digital age, seeking connection and companionship in an ever-changing landscape. We delve into the deep human desire for love and companionship, highlighting the significance of relationships in Christian life. The pursuit of meaningful connections is universal, transcending time and culture, and it's a quest that many Christians embark on with devotion and prayer.

Section 2: The Changing Landscape

Here, we explore how the landscape of singleness and dating has evolved over the years. From traditional courtship to modern dating apps, we examine the influences of technology, globalization, and shifting cultural norms on the way Christians meet and interact. We acknowledge the challenges of adapting to these changes while maintaining one's faith and values.

Section 3: The Intersection of Faith and Love

A Christian's pursuit of love is intricately woven with their faith. In this section, we delve into the significance of faith in shaping one's approach to dating and relationships. We discuss the principles and values that guide Christian singles, focusing on the importance of faith compatibility, shared values, and a Christ-centered foundation for a lasting relationship.

Section 4: Embracing Singleness

We explore the concept of singleness as a season of life to be embraced and celebrated. Drawing from biblical and historical examples, we highlight the unique opportunities and blessings that come with being single. Whether it's dedicated service, self-discovery, or personal growth, this section encourages readers to view their singleness as a gift rather than a waiting period.

Section 5: Challenges and Opportunities

This section addresses the real challenges that modern Christian singles face in today's dating landscape. Loneliness, peer pressure, and the pressure to conform to worldly standards are discussed, along with practical advice on navigating these hurdles. It also offers insights into the opportunities presented by modern dating, emphasizing the power of intentionality and faith-driven choices.

Section 6: Setting the Stage

To conclude the chapter, we set the stage for the journey ahead. We discuss the purpose of this book, which is to provide guidance, support, and encouragement for Christian singles navigating the complexities of modern dating. We introduce the core themes that will be explored in the upcoming chapters, such as faith-based dating principles, communication skills, and embracing a Christ-centered approach.

Chapter 1 serves as a foundation for the book, laying out the context, challenges, and opportunities that Christian singles face in the modern age. It also sets the tone for a thoughtful and faith-driven exploration of Christian dating in a digital, fast-paced world, with a focus on embracing singleness and seeking love within the boundaries of Christian faith.

2

Navigating Singleness: A Season of Growth

In this chapter of "Navigating Singleness: Christian Dating for the Modern Age," we delve into the concept of singleness as a season of growth, self-discovery, and spiritual development. We explore the ways in which Christian singles can make the most of this season, preparing themselves for meaningful and faith-driven relationships.

Section 1: The Purpose of Singleness

We begin by discussing the profound purpose behind the season of singleness, drawing from both biblical and contemporary perspectives. Through stories and scripture, we illustrate how singleness can be a time of unique devotion to God, personal growth, and self-discovery. By framing singleness as an opportunity rather than a limitation, we encourage readers to embrace this season with a sense of purpose.

Section 2: Developing a Strong Relationship with God

The foundation of any successful Christian dating journey is a strong personal relationship with God. This section explores how singles can use their season of singleness to deepen their faith, nurture their spirituality, and establish a strong connection with God. Practical tips, including prayer and Bible study routines, are discussed to help readers grow in their faith.

Section 3: Self-Discovery and Personal Growth

Singleness offers an excellent opportunity for self-discovery and personal growth. We delve into the importance of knowing oneself, identifying personal goals, and developing one's interests and talents. Through anecdotes and exercises, we guide readers in understanding their unique qualities, which can ultimately enhance their future relationships.

Section 4: Emotional and Spiritual Healing

Many Christian singles come to their season of singleness with past wounds and baggage. This section focuses on the healing process, both emotionally and spiritually. Strategies for forgiveness, letting go of past relationships, and seeking emotional wholeness are explored, allowing readers to approach future relationships with a healthier perspective.

Section 5: Community and Support

Singleness doesn't have to be a lonely journey. We discuss the importance of surrounding oneself with a supportive Christian community. This includes involvement in church activities, small groups, and friendships that can provide encouragement and accountability. We emphasize the idea that singleness is not about being alone but rather about being in a different kind of community.

Section 6: Setting Relationship Goals

As readers grow in their singleness, it's important to set relationship goals that align with their faith and values. We explore how to define these goals and the significance of seeking compatibility in these areas. Practical exercises and insights are provided to help readers set clear intentions for future relationships.

Section 7: Preparing for a Christ-Centered Relationship

In the final part of this chapter, we lay the groundwork for the journey ahead. We discuss the value of a Christ-centered relationship, focusing on the importance of shared values, communication, and spiritual connection. We set the stage for the subsequent chapters, which will delve deeper into the practical aspects of Christian dating for the modern age.

Chapter 2 serves as a guide to making the most of the season of singleness, highlighting its purpose and potential for personal growth, spiritual development, and healing. It encourages readers to see singleness as a season filled with opportunities and prepares them for the practical aspects of navigating Christian dating in the modern age.

3

Faith-Driven Dating Principles

In "Navigating Singleness: Christian Dating for the Modern Age," this chapter explores the foundational principles that underpin Christian dating. It provides a comprehensive framework for Christian singles seeking to navigate the complexities of modern dating while staying true to their faith.

Section 1: The Foundation of Faith

We begin by emphasizing the paramount importance of faith in Christian dating. This section dives deep into the foundational role of faith in forming and sustaining a Christ-centered relationship. It touches upon key scriptures and teachings that guide Christian dating principles, encouraging readers to anchor their search for love in their faith.

Section 2: Purity and Integrity

Maintaining purity and integrity in relationships is a fundamental principle of Christian dating. We discuss the biblical concept of purity in mind, body, and spirit, and the importance of maintaining integrity in one's actions and intentions. Practical advice on setting boundaries and fostering a culture of respect is offered to readers.

Section 3: Emotional and Spiritual Connection

This section delves into the significance of emotional and spiritual connection as the bedrock of a faith-driven relationship. We explore how emotional intimacy can be developed through meaningful communication, vulnerability, and shared experiences. Additionally, we discuss the importance of spiritual alignment, wherein couples grow together in their faith.

Section 4: Honesty and Transparency

Honesty and transparency are values that are non-negotiable in Christian dating. We elaborate on the importance of open and honest communication, even when it's difficult. This section also addresses issues such as dealing with past mistakes and making amends, emphasizing the transformative power of truth and reconciliation.

Section 5: Respect and Dignity

In this section, we emphasize the Christian value of respecting the dignity of every individual. We discuss how to treat one another with kindness and honor, regardless of the stage of the relationship. The principle of mutual respect is central to maintaining healthy and Christ-centered partnerships.

Section 6: Purpose-Driven Dating

The concept of purpose-driven dating is introduced, which involves discerning the purpose and goals of the relationship and ensuring that they align with one's faith. We discuss how to set shared goals, navigate differences, and discern whether the relationship is heading in the right direction.

Section 7: Trusting God's Timing

The chapter concludes by addressing the challenge of patience in the search for love. We explore the idea that trusting God's timing is fundamental to Christian dating, even when it feels like a season of waiting. This section provides guidance on handling the desire for a relationship while keeping faith in God's plan.

Chapter 3 offers Christian singles a strong foundation of faith-driven dating principles. It outlines the values and practices essential for nurturing healthy, purposeful, and Christ-centered relationships in the modern age. This chapter equips readers with the knowledge and understanding needed to navigate the challenges of dating while upholding their faith.

4

Communication and Connection

In this chapter of "Navigating Singleness: Christian Dating for the Modern Age," we delve into the essential skills and practices related to communication and connection in the context of Christian dating. Effective communication is the lifeblood of any relationship, and this chapter equips readers with the tools and insights to foster meaningful connections while upholding their faith.

Section 1: The Power of Communication

We begin by highlighting the transformative power of communication in relationships. Effective communication is vital for understanding, empathy, and resolving conflicts. We emphasize the role of communication in building trust and connection while remaining grounded in Christian values.

Section 2: Active Listening and Empathy

Active listening and empathy are explored as cornerstones of effective communication. We provide practical tips and techniques for improving one's listening skills, demonstrating empathy, and understanding a partner's perspective. The Christian value of compassion and understanding is reinforced.

Section 3: Healthy Conflict Resolution

Conflict is an inevitable part of any relationship, and in this section, we delve into how Christian singles can approach conflict resolution with grace and respect. We discuss strategies for addressing disagreements in a healthy and productive manner, emphasizing the importance of maintaining a Christ-centered focus.

Section 4: Navigating Modern Communication Tools

With the advent of technology, modern dating often involves a range of communication tools, from texting to social media. We explore the benefits and challenges of these tools, offering advice on how to use them effectively while maintaining boundaries and respect for one another.

Section 5: Communicating Faith and Values

Openly discussing faith and values is crucial in Christian dating. This section guides readers on how to engage in meaningful conversations about their faith, beliefs, and values with a potential partner. We provide insights into fostering a shared spiritual connection.

Section 6: Building Emotional Intimacy

Christian dating is about more than just physical attraction; it's about building deep emotional connections. We discuss strategies for developing emotional intimacy through vulnerability, shared experiences, and meaningful conversations. We also emphasize the importance of maintaining boundaries in this process.

Section 7: Prayer and Spiritual Connection

Prayer is a powerful tool in Christian dating. This section explores how couples can develop a strong spiritual connection through prayer together. We provide guidance on integrating prayer into the relationship and seeking God's guidance as a couple.

Section 8: Honoring Boundaries

Boundaries are essential in Christian dating to protect one's physical and emotional well-being. We discuss the importance of setting clear boundaries and respecting each other's limits. Practical advice on boundary-setting is offered to help readers navigate this aspect of Christian dating.

Section 9: The Art of Romance

Romance is a beautiful aspect of Christian dating, and we explore how to infuse romance into the relationship while adhering to Christian values. We discuss date ideas, gestures of love, and ways to keep the romance alive.

Chapter 4 equips readers with the knowledge and skills necessary for effective communication and connection in the context of Christian dating. It reinforces the importance of empathy, active listening, and conflict resolution, all while maintaining faith-based values. This chapter ensures that Christian singles can foster deep, meaningful connections as they navigate the modern dating landscape.

5

Navigating the Digital World of Dating

In "Navigating Singleness: Christian Dating for the Modern Age," this chapter explores the unique challenges and opportunities presented by the digital world of dating. As technology continues to shape how people meet and connect, Christian singles must navigate this landscape while staying true to their faith.

Section 1: The Digital Dating Landscape

This section sets the stage by examining the impact of digital technology on modern dating. We discuss the proliferation of dating apps, websites, and online platforms, and how they have transformed the dating experience. It acknowledges the opportunities and challenges digital dating presents.

Section 2: Maintaining Christian Values Online

The core of this section delves into how Christian singles can navigate online dating while staying true to their values. It explores the importance of honesty, transparency, and integrity in online profiles and conversations. Readers will learn how to discern potential partners' values and faith alignment in a digital context.

Section 3: Online Safety and Boundaries

Online dating brings its own set of safety concerns. We discuss strategies for ensuring personal safety and the importance of setting and respecting online boundaries. This section also addresses potential pitfalls like catfishing, and how to identify and respond to red flags.

Section 4: The Art of Online Communication

Online communication is different from in-person interaction. This section provides guidance on how to initiate and maintain meaningful conversations in a digital context. It explores the balance of text-based communication and maintaining the depth of emotional connection.

Section 5: Managing Expectations

Online dating often comes with a variety of expectations, both realistic and idealized. We discuss how to manage these expectations and understand that the digital world may not always reflect reality. It's important for Christian singles to stay grounded and true to their faith as they navigate this landscape.

Section 6: Balancing Online and Offline Dating

While online dating is a prevalent avenue for meeting potential partners, it's important to strike a balance with offline interactions. We explore how Christian singles can transition from online communication to in-person meetings, emphasizing the importance of face-to-face connections.

Section 7: The Role of Friends and Family

Friends and family can play a crucial role in helping Christian singles navigate the digital world of dating. We discuss the value of seeking advice and accountability from trusted loved ones and how they can help assess potential partners and relationships.

Section 8: Staying Christ-Centered in Digital Dating

The chapter concludes by reinforcing the importance of keeping Christ at the center of the dating journey, whether online or offline. We provide practical guidance on how to maintain faith-based values and priorities while navigating the digital world of dating.

Chapter 5 equips readers with the knowledge and skills necessary to navigate the digital world of dating while adhering to Christian values. It addresses the unique challenges presented by online dating, provides strategies for maintaining integrity, and underscores the importance of keeping Christ at the center of the dating experience. This chapter ensures that Christian singles can confidently explore the digital landscape while staying grounded in their faith.

6

Preparing for a Christ-Centered Relationship

In "Navigating Singleness: Christian Dating for the Modern Age," this chapter explores the crucial stage of preparing for a Christ-centered relationship. It is a time of anticipation and readiness, where Christian singles actively seek to find a partner with whom they can share a purpose-driven, faith-based relationship.

Section 1: The Power of Preparation

This section emphasizes the importance of preparing for a Christ-centered relationship. It explains how a strong foundation is essential before embarking on this new journey, just as a builder needs a solid base before constructing a house.

Section 2: Self-Reflection and Self-Improvement

To prepare for a Christ-centered relationship, individuals must reflect upon their own character and values. This section provides guidance on self-assessment and personal development, ensuring that readers are continually working towards becoming the best version of themselves.

Section 3: Establishing Relationship Goals

Successful relationships require clear goals. This section guides readers through the process of establishing relationship goals and understanding what they desire in a partner, both spiritually and personally.

Section 4: Honoring God in the Waiting

For many Christian singles, the preparation stage can be marked by waiting for the right partner. This section explores how to honor God in the waiting, maintain patience, and continue to grow in faith and purpose during this season.

Section 5: Redefining Relationship Expectations

Preparing for a Christ-centered relationship often involves reevaluating and redefining expectations. This section discusses the importance of aligning expectations with Christian values and being open to the unexpected.

Section 6: The Role of Community

Community support is a valuable resource during the preparation stage. This section highlights the importance of seeking guidance and accountability from trusted friends, family, and mentors who can help individuals in their preparation journey.

Section 7: Keeping God at the Center

The chapter concludes by reiterating the importance of keeping God at the center of the preparation process. Readers are encouraged to maintain their faith and rely on God's guidance as they prepare for a Christ-centered relationship.

Chapter 6 equips readers with the tools and mindset necessary to prepare for a Christ-centered relationship. It emphasizes self-reflection, goal-setting, and the significance of community support during this crucial stage. By keeping God at the center of the preparation journey, Christian singles can position themselves for a meaningful, faith-driven relationship in the modern age.

7

Embracing Love: Entering a Christ-Centered Relationship

In "Navigating Singleness: Christian Dating for the Modern Age," this chapter delves into the transition from singleness to a Christ-centered relationship. It explores the excitement, challenges, and steps involved in entering a new phase of life marked by love, faith, and companionship.

Section 1: The Joy of Connection

We begin by celebrating the joy of connecting with a potential partner who shares similar values and faith. This section explores the excitement and gratitude that come with finding someone who aligns with one's spiritual journey.

Section 2: Building a Strong Foundation

Entering a Christ-centered relationship requires a solid foundation. We discuss how to establish a strong base through open communication, mutual respect, and shared goals. Readers will learn about the importance of a Christ-centered approach and fostering a shared spiritual connection.

Section 3: Defining the Relationship

The definition of the relationship is a critical step. We explore the importance of defining the relationship's boundaries and goals, helping readers navigate the transition from casual dating to a committed, faith-driven partnership.

Section 4: The Role of Friends and Family

Friends and family play a significant role in this transition. We discuss how to involve loved ones, seek their advice and support, and ensure that they are part of the celebration of this new phase in life.

Section 5: Challenges in a Christ-Centered Relationship

Every relationship faces challenges. This section addresses common challenges encountered in Christ-centered relationships, including faith-based disagreements, differing expectations, and maintaining a balance between individual and shared goals.

Section 6: Nurturing Love and Faith

Love and faith are intertwined in a Christ-centered relationship. This section provides insights into how couples can nurture their love while deepening their faith through shared experiences, spiritual practices, and prayer.

Section 7: Overcoming Obstacles Together

In any relationship, there will be obstacles to overcome. This section offers guidance on facing challenges as a team, drawing on faith and love to find solutions and grow stronger together.

Section 8: Celebrating Milestones

Milestones in a relationship, such as anniversaries and significant events, provide opportunities for celebration and reflection. This section discusses how to honor these moments and build lasting memories grounded in faith.

Section 9: Keeping God at the Center

The chapter concludes by reinforcing the importance of keeping God at the center of the relationship. Readers are encouraged to continue seeking God's guidance and wisdom as they navigate the complexities and joys of a Christ-centered relationship.

Chapter 7 offers readers a comprehensive guide to transitioning from singleness to a Christ-centered relationship. It provides insights into defining the relationship, addressing challenges, nurturing love and faith, and celebrating important milestones. Throughout this chapter, the message of keeping God at the center is reinforced, ensuring that the relationship remains firmly grounded in faith.

8

A Future Together: Preparing for Commitment

In "Navigating Singleness: Christian Dating for the Modern Age," this chapter explores the next stage in a Christ-centered relationship: the path to commitment. It addresses the steps and considerations involved in moving towards a future together marked by faith, love, and devotion.

Section 1: The Call to Commitment

The chapter begins by discussing the significance of commitment in a Christ-centered relationship. It explores the concept of a life together, sharing a future, and the call to make a deeper commitment to one another.

Section 2: Discerning God's Plan

Discerning God's plan for the relationship is crucial. This section emphasizes the importance of seeking God's guidance, through prayer and reflection, to ensure that the relationship aligns with His will.

Section 3: Preparing for a Lifelong Covenant

A lifelong commitment often leads to the covenant of marriage. We delve into the preparations needed for marriage, including discussions about the sacrament of marriage and the commitment to a covenant-based relationship.

Section 4: Building a Strong Partnership

The foundation for a Christ-centered commitment is a strong partnership. This section provides insights into building a partnership based on mutual respect, open communication, and shared values. It emphasizes the importance of teamwork and trust.

Section 5: Preparing for Challenges

Commitment involves facing challenges together. This section addresses the potential difficulties that may arise in the future and offers strategies for preparing for and addressing them as a couple.

Section 6: Seeking Support and Guidance

Seeking support from a faith community and trusted mentors is invaluable. We discuss how couples can involve their church, pastor, or spiritual mentors in their journey toward commitment.

Section 7: Honoring Commitment and Purity

This section underscores the importance of maintaining purity and honor in the relationship as it moves towards commitment. It discusses the biblical principles of purity and how they apply to a Christ-centered commitment.

Section 8: Engagement and Wedding Planning

For many couples, the commitment phase includes an engagement and wedding planning. We provide guidance on these significant steps and offer advice on how to approach them with faith and love in mind.

Section 9: Keeping God at the Center of Commitment

The chapter concludes by emphasizing that, even as couples move toward commitment, keeping God at the center of their relationship remains paramount. It highlights the importance of continued faith and reliance on God's guidance as the relationship advances.

Chapter 8 equips readers with the knowledge and guidance needed to prepare for a lifelong commitment in a Christ-centered relationship. It addresses discerning God's plan, building a strong partnership, and preparing for challenges and milestones. The chapter ensures that couples are ready to take the next step in their faith-driven journey together.

9

A Christ-Centered Marriage

In "Navigating Singleness: Christian Dating for the Modern Age," this chapter focuses on the realization of a Christ-centered marriage, marking the culmination of a faith-driven journey of love, commitment, and partnership.

Section 1: The Sacred Covenant of Marriage

The chapter begins by discussing the sacred covenant of marriage from a Christian perspective. It explores the biblical foundations of marriage, highlighting the profound spiritual significance of this commitment.

Section 2: Preparing for Marriage

Before entering into a Christ-centered marriage, couples need to take practical steps to prepare. This section addresses the importance of pre-marital counseling, financial planning, and establishing a shared vision for the future.

Section 3: The Marriage Ceremony

The wedding ceremony is a pivotal moment in the journey toward a Christ-centered marriage. This section discusses how to plan a wedding that reflects the couple's faith and values, emphasizing the importance of inviting God's presence into the celebration.

Section 4: The Role of Community and Accountability

Community support and accountability remain vital, even in the context of marriage. This section discusses how couples can involve their church community and trusted mentors in their marriage and how accountability can help strengthen the marital bond.

Section 5: Spiritual Leadership in Marriage

Christian marriages require spiritual leadership. This section explores the roles of husband and wife in a faith-centered marriage and how they can jointly lead their family in faith and love.

Section 6: Navigating Challenges in Marriage

Every marriage faces challenges. This section provides guidance on how couples can navigate and overcome these obstacles with faith, patience, and open communication.

Section 7: Marriage Enrichment and Growth

Marriage is not static but a journey of growth and enrichment. This section discusses how couples can continually nurture their relationship through spiritual practices, shared experiences, and the pursuit of shared goals.

Section 8: Keeping God at the Center of Marriage

The chapter concludes by reiterating the importance of keeping God at the center of the marriage. It underscores the continued reliance on faith and the guidance of the Divine as couples journey through the complexities and joys of a Christ-centered marriage.

Chapter 9 equips readers with the knowledge and insights needed to embrace a Christ-centered marriage fully. It addresses the sacred nature of the marital covenant, preparations, the wedding ceremony, and the ongoing growth and challenges that come with marriage. This chapter ensures that couples can continue to navigate their lives together in alignment with their Christian faith and values.

10

Building a Christ-Centered Family

In "Navigating Singleness: Christian Dating for the Modern Age," this chapter explores the next chapter in the journey: building a Christ-centered family. It delves into the foundational aspects of raising a family rooted in faith, love, and Christian values.

Section 1: The Christian Family Vision

This section introduces the concept of a Christian family vision. It discusses the importance of having a shared vision as a couple, outlining values, goals, and the role of faith in raising a family.

Section 2: Parenthood and Faith

Parenthood is a significant responsibility. This section addresses how Christian parents can integrate faith into their parenting, from teaching spiritual values to fostering a love for God in their children.

Section 3: Building a Faithful Home

Creating a faithful home is essential in a Christ-centered family. This section explores practical ways to make the home a place where faith is nurtured through daily routines, prayer, and spiritual traditions.

Section 4: Nurturing Faith in Children

Nurturing faith in children is a continuous process. The chapter discusses how to guide children in their spiritual journeys, answer their questions, and encourage them to develop a personal relationship with God.

Section 5: Family Devotions and Worship

The family's faith is strengthened through regular devotions and worship. This section provides guidance on how families can establish and maintain devotional practices and worship that reflect their Christian beliefs.

Section 6: Education and Faith

Education plays a pivotal role in a Christian family. This section explores how to select schools, curricula, and extracurricular activities that align with Christian values and contribute to the holistic development of children.

Section 7: Family Challenges and Resilience

Challenges are inevitable in family life. This section addresses common family challenges and provides strategies for fostering resilience, unity, and faith-based solutions.

Section 8: Community and Support

A strong support system is invaluable in the journey of building a Christ-centered family. This section discusses the importance of being involved in a faith community, connecting with like-minded families, and seeking guidance from mentors.

Section 9: Maintaining a Christ-Centered Marriage

The foundation of a Christ-centered family is a Christ-centered marriage. This section underscores the need to maintain a strong marital bond, even while raising a family, and discusses strategies for preserving the couple's relationship.

Section 10: Keeping God at the Center

The chapter concludes by reiterating the importance of keeping God at the center of the family. It emphasizes that faith remains the guiding light for the family's values, decisions, and the journey of building a Christ-centered home.

Chapter 10 equips readers with the knowledge and guidance necessary to build and nurture a Christ-centered family. It addresses the family vision, parenthood, home environment, nurturing faith in children, and the challenges families may face. The chapter ensures that Christian families can navigate the complexities and joys of family life while keeping God at the core of their journey.

11

The Legacy of Faith

In "Navigating Singleness: Christian Dating for the Modern Age," this chapter explores the idea of leaving a lasting legacy of faith. It delves into the significance of passing down faith, values, and the Christian way of life to the next generation.

Section 1: The Power of a Faith Legacy

The chapter opens by discussing the profound impact of a faith legacy. It explores the importance of leaving behind a spiritual inheritance that can shape the lives of future generations.

Section 2: Teaching and Modeling Faith

Passing down faith starts with teaching and modeling. This section provides insights into how Christian parents and grandparents can teach the next generation about God, prayer, scripture, and living a life grounded in faith.

Section 3: Celebrating Traditions and Milestones

Family traditions and milestone celebrations are a vital part of a faith legacy. The chapter discusses how Christian families can establish traditions that reflect their beliefs and make important milestones in a person's spiritual journey.

Section 4: Mentoring and Discipleship

Mentoring and discipleship are essential in nurturing faith. This section explores the role of mentors, both within and outside the family, in guiding and inspiring the next generation in their faith journey.

Section 5: Christian Education and Community

Choosing a Christian education and being part of a faith community can significantly impact the development of faith in the next generation. This section discusses the importance of making intentional choices in these areas.

Section 6: Embracing Generational Diversity

Families often consist of individuals of various ages and stages of faith. This section explores the significance of embracing generational diversity and how it can enrich the faith legacy.

Section 7: Navigating Challenges in Legacy Building

Building a faith legacy may come with challenges. This section addresses common obstacles and provides strategies for navigating them while staying true to one's values.

Section 8: Keeping God at the Center

The chapter concludes by reiterating the importance of keeping God at the center of the effort to build a faith legacy. It emphasizes that faith is the foundation upon which a lasting legacy is built.

Chapter 11 equips readers with the knowledge and guidance necessary to leave a lasting legacy of faith. It addresses teaching, modeling, traditions, mentoring, and the challenges that may arise in the process. The chapter ensures that Christian families can navigate the complexities of legacy building while keeping God at the core of their efforts.

12

An Ever-Evolving Journey

In "Navigating Singleness: Christian Dating for the Modern Age," this chapter explores the idea that the journey of faith and relationships is ever-evolving. It emphasizes the need for continuous growth, adaptation, and reliance on God's guidance in every stage of life.

Section 1: Embracing Change

The chapter begins by discussing the inevitability of change in life, relationships, and faith. It highlights the importance of embracing change with a spirit of faith and adaptability.

Section 2: Lifelong Learning

Continuous learning and growth are essential aspects of a faith journey. This section provides insights into how individuals and couples can engage in lifelong learning, from studying scripture to seeking new perspectives.

Section 3: Balancing Faith, Family, and Career

Balancing faith, family, and career is a complex task. The chapter explores strategies for individuals and couples to find harmony in these important areas of life while keeping their faith at the center.

Section 4: Navigating Parenthood

Parenthood is a new phase that comes with its own set of challenges and joys. This section addresses the transition to parenthood and the importance of nurturing faith within the family.

Section 5: Relying on God's Guidance

Relying on God's guidance remains a constant in the ever-evolving journey of faith and relationships. This section underscores the importance of seeking God's direction in every stage of life.

Section 6: Revisiting the Past

Reflecting on the past and learning from one's experiences is a crucial part of the journey. This section discusses how revisiting the past can offer valuable insights for the present and future.

Section 7: Fostering Faith in the Next Generation

The journey also involves passing down faith to the next generation. This section offers insights into how to be intentional in fostering faith in children and grandchildren.

Section 8: Embracing a Christ-Centered Marriage

For couples, maintaining a Christ-centered marriage remains a priority. This section provides guidance on keeping love and faith at the core of the marital relationship.

Section 9: Keeping God at the Center

The chapter concludes by reiterating the enduring importance of keeping God at the center of every stage of the ever-evolving journey. It emphasizes that faith remains the guiding force in adapting to change, learning, and growing in life and relationships.

Chapter 12 equips readers with the understanding that the journey of faith and relationships is continuous and ever-evolving. It addresses change, lifelong learning, balancing life's various facets, and the importance of relying on God's guidance. This chapter ensures that individuals and couples can navigate the complexities of their ever-evolving journey while keeping God at the heart of it all.

Title: Navigating Singleness: Christian Dating for the Modern Age

Book Summary:

"Navigating Singleness: Christian Dating for the Modern Age" is an insightful guide that explores the intricate journey of faith-driven relationships in contemporary times. Through twelve comprehensive chapters, the book provides a holistic approach to Christian dating, incorporating biblical wisdom, practical advice, and spiritual guidance.

The book begins by redefining singleness, emphasizing its potential for personal growth and self-discovery. It invites readers to embrace this season with purpose and devotion to God, preparing them for the challenges and joys of modern Christian dating.

Each chapter builds upon the last, guiding readers through the various stages of this journey:

- Faith-Driven Dating Principles: This chapter establishes the fundamental principles that underpin Christian dating, emphasizing purity, emotional and spiritual connection, honesty, and transparency.

- Communication and Connection: Effective communication is the lifeblood of any relationship, and this chapter equips readers with the tools and insights to foster meaningful connections while upholding their faith.

- The Digital World of Dating: Modern dating often involves online platforms and apps. This chapter addresses the challenges and opportunities presented by the digital world of dating while staying true to Christian values.

- Preparing for a Christ-Centered Relationship: Preparation is key to a successful relationship. This chapter guides readers through self-reflection, relationship goal-setting, and understanding the purpose of the relationship.

- Entering a Christ-Centered Relationship: Transitioning from singleness to a Christ-centered relationship is a momentous step. This chapter explores building a strong foundation, defining the relationship, and involving the community.

- Preparing for Commitment: As the relationship deepens, this chapter addresses the practical steps needed to prepare for commitment, including counseling and financial planning.

- A Christ-Centered Marriage: The wedding ceremony and the first years of marriage are explored in this chapter, emphasizing the importance of a Christ-centered marriage.

- Building a Christ-Centered Family: Nurturing a faith-driven family is the focus here, from establishing a family vision to teaching and modeling faith for children.

- The Legacy of Faith: This chapter discusses the significance of leaving a lasting legacy of faith for future generations, exploring teaching, mentoring, and faith traditions.

- An Ever-Evolving Journey: The book concludes by emphasizing the ever-evolving nature of the faith and relationship journey. It encourages readers to embrace change, lifelong learning, and continuous reliance on God's guidance.

Throughout the book, the central message is to keep God at the core of every aspect of the journey, whether single, dating, married, or nurturing a family. "Navigating Singleness" is a comprehensive resource that equips readers to navigate the complexities and joys of faith-driven relationships in the modern age. It reinforces the idea that Christian values and faith can be unwavering guides in every stage of life and love.

www.ingramcontent.com/pod-product-compliance
Lightning Source LLC
LaVergne TN
LVHW020456080526
838202LV00057B/5978